Words to the Wise

by Freddie Bell

Dedication

This book is dedicated to my wife, Francine, my
children Jasmine, and Jahreya,
my granddaughter, Zoey and to friends, family,
and fans who have listened to
my programs over the years.

About Freddie Bell

Freddie Bell is General Manager of KMOJ-FM HD1; The People's Station and KMOJ FM HD2; The Ice. Prior to joining KMOJ in 2014, Freddie was General Manager of The Twin Cities Totally Gospel Radio Network and CBS's AM 950, Solid Gold Soul based in Edina, MN.

Bell manages and hosts three radio programs, two of which air in the Twin Cities and the third across the country in syndication. He is also a public speaker under his SGS Entertainment Company.

Focusing on government and education, Bell began his professional career as a television broadcast-journalist for ABC News affiliate, KETV in Omaha, NE, and has worked in markets including, Tampa, and the Nation's Capital.

Freddie Bell, popular speaker – successful author (Wise Words and Affirmations CD), is a pervasive presence on radio and a welcome motivational orator at corporations and non-profit institutions on topics including "The Secrets of Community Radio Management," Maximizing Your Potential, The Power of Focus, and "Successful Selling Techniques."

In speaking engagements Freddie Bell affords invaluable insight gleaned from his work in media.

Freddie Bell shares ideas on how to maximize your potential, and how to lead a vibrant, healthy, and profoundly productive life through the Power of Focus in business and professionally.

The Freddie Bell Show is syndicated to nearly 20 stations nationally, showcasing music, feature stories and artist profiles.

The award-winning host of CBS Radio's Solid Gold Soul welcomes guests to New Beginnings (KTNF-AM, 950) addresses employment and topics important to a wide range of listeners.

Highlighted on The Freddie Bell Show and New Beginnings is his forum, "Power of Focus." It features in-depth interviews designed to encourage and inspire people to realize their full potential

The Morning Show with Freddie Bell and Chantel Sings is heard over the Twin Cites airwaves via KMOJ, broadcasting popular music and scintillating conversation to a widely diverse audience.

Introduction

Words to the Wise began as a daily message on my radio morning show program in the mid-nineties in Minnesota. I worked for a CBS radio station that was housed in a small, converted house in Eden Prairie, MN. The station, 950 AM, KSGS featured an Urban Oldies music format, called Solid Gold Soul, featuring Motown and classic soul hits originated in the 1960s and the 1970s.

As Station Manager and host of that local Morning Show, the usually one-sentence messages, called Words to the Wise, were developed from my reaction to articles I had read recently, shows I had seen on television, or were ideas generated from life experiences.

In mid-2014, I joined KMOJ-FM as a co-host of its Morning Show in Minneapolis after working in other markets around the country. I revived the Words to The Wise in hopes it would not only reconnect me with former listeners, but also to speak encouragement to those who listen now.

While there are 366 Words to the Wise, the messages are not necessarily meant to be read day-by-day. You can literally open the book to any passage and be fed by the wisdom of the thought found on that page. It may be that you use the same Word to the Wise each day or several times a day. You decide.

The idea is for the wisdom of the words to feed your mind, body, and spirit. If you are moved by the words, and they become part of you, then my goal for you has been accomplished.

Words to the Wise

Patience

Here are today's Words to the Wise.
"I radiate patience and joy
in all my affairs today."

Capacity

Here are today's Words to the Wise.
"You can only do what you can do."

Progress

Here are today's Words to the Wise.
"Keep on Truckin!"

Power

Here are today's Words to the Wise.
"I am empowered to express
the essence of who I am."

Courage

Here are today's Words to the Wise.
"I press on, even when
the outcome isn't clear."

Glow

Here are today's Words to the Wise.
"We always have an abundance
of internal sunshine."

True Identity

Here are today's Words to the Wise.
"Strive to live your truth each day."

Confidence

Here are today's Words to the Wise.
"Take a leap of faith."

Wisdom

Here are today's Words to the Wise.
"The past is a great judge of the future."

Fortune

Here are today's Words to the Wise.
"Don't tempt fate."

Kissing Day

Here are today's Words to the Wise.
"Share a kiss with a special person."

Giggle

Here are today's Words to the Wise.
"Express Your Joy Through Laughter."

Success

Here are today's Words to the Wise.
"Life is a journey."

Inner Beauty

Here are today's Words to the Wise.
"Allow your joy to shine!"

Awareness

Here are today's Words to the Wise.
"Recognize opportunities."

Empathy

Here are today's Words to the Wise!
"Don't fuel the fire."

Goals

Here are today's Words to the Wise.
"Go for it!"

Gifts

Here are today's Words to the Wise.
"Children are among our greatest blessings."

Encouragement

Here are today's Words to the Wise.
"Be an inspiration with
your words and actions."

Mightily Made

Here are today's Words to the Wise.
"Greatness is in each one of us."

Focus

Here are today's Words to the Wise.
"Live your life with positive expectancy."

Wealth

Here are today's Words to the Wise.
"Knowing when you have
enough is to be rich."

Achievement

Here are today's Words to the Wise.
"It's easier to keep up than to catch up."

Blessing

Here are today's Words to the Wise.
"Look for opportunities to
be someone's miracle."

Wise

Here are today's Words to the Wise.
"Enemies keep us on our toes."

Sharing

Here are today's Words to the Wise.
"Allow your compassionate heart to show."

Happiness

Here are today's Words to the Wise.
"Every day is a reason to celebrate."

Success

Here are today's Words to the Wise.
"You are born to succeed."

Integrity

Here are today's Words to the Wise.
"You are what you do."

Expectations

Here are today's Words to Wise.
"See the best in people."

Giving

Here are today's Words to the Wise.
"It's not how much we give, it's how much love
we put into giving." —Mother Teresa

Integrity

Here are today's Words to the Wise.
"Be the example."

Priorities

Here are today's Words to the Wise.
"Focus on what matters most."

True Joy

Here are today's Words to the Wise.
"Choose to be joyous today."

Achievement

Here are today's Words to the Wise.
"Progress always has a cost."

Family

Here are today's Words to the Wise.
"Make your house a home."

Wisdom

Here are today's Words to the Wise.
"Know when to ask for help."

Self-Reliance

Here are today's Words to the Wise.
"Challenge yourself."

Value

Here are today's Words to the Wise.
"Every little bit counts."

Real Beauty

Here are today's Words to the Wise.
"Inner beauty will last longer
than outer beauty!"

Freedom

Here are today's Words to the Wise.
"We as a people will get to the promised land."
—Dr. Martin Luther King Jr.

Start

Here are today's Words to the Wise.
"Begin at the Beginning."

Strength

Here are today's Words to the Wise.
"You are mightily made."

Resolve

Here are today's Words to the Wise.
"It can be tough, but
face adversity with a smile."

Reflection

Here are today's Words to the Wise.
"Discover your purpose."

Fortitude

Here are today's Words to the Wise.
"You're well able to handle difficult times."

Abundant Living

Here are today's Words to the Wise.
"Live a life of honesty and integrity."

Trust

Here are today's Words to the Wise.
"Believe in something greater than yourself."

Wisdom

Here are today's Words to the Wise.
"Trust your judgement."

Belief

Here are today's Words to the Wise.
"We are what we believe."

Expectation

Here are today's Words to the Wise.
"Actively look for the good."

Belief

Here are today's Words to the Wise.
"All things are possible if you believe."

Well-Being

Here are today's Words to the Wise.
"Good health is priceless."

Awareness

Here are today's Words to the Wise.
"The unexpected always happens."

Education

Here are today's Words to the Wise.
"Ignorance is expensive."

Direction

Here are today's Words to the Wise.
"Know where you're going."

Tough

Here are today's Words to the Wise
"Give it one more try."

Heart

Here are today's Words to the Wise.
"Eyes are the windows of the soul."

Persevere

Here are today's Words to the Wise.
"Don't stop trying during trying times."

Thankful

Here are today's Words to the Wise.
"Be in a constant state of thanksgiving."

Inner Beauty

Here are today's Words to the Wise.
"Beauty is in everyone. Take a good look."

Integrity

Here are today's Words to the Wise.
"A lie can never become the truth."

Prompt

Here are today's Words to the Wise.
"Be on time."

Lift Your Voice

Here are today's Words to the Wise.
"Singing warms the heart."

Even More Joy

Here are today's Words to the Wise.
"Joy shared is doubled."

Joy

Here are today's Words to the Wise.
"Life is a song to sing."

Wisdom

Here are today's Words to the Wise.
"Give it a Second Thought!"

Reality Check

Here are today's Words to the Wise.
"Things are not always as they seem."

Self-Care

Here are today's Words to the Wise.
"Pamper yourself now and then."

Joy

Here are today's Words to the Wise.
"Let your heart sing."

Inspiration

Here are today's Words to the Wise.
"Inspire Hope."

Giving

Here are today's Words to the Wise.
"Be a Miracle."

Belief

Here are today's Words to the Wise.
"There's always a way, some way."

Pride

Here are today's Words to the Wise.
"Say it Loud!!"

Faith

Here are today's Words to the Wise.
"Only believe."

Hard Work

Here are today's Words to the Wise.
"Elbow grease gives the best polish."

Education

Here are today's Words to the Wise.
"Reading is exercise for the mind."

Knowledge

Here are today's Words to the Wise.
"Reading is exercise for the mind."

Joy

Here are today's Words to the Wise.
"Happiness is where you find it."

Joy

Here are today's Words to the Wise.
"Let your heart sing!"

Attitude

Here are today's Words to the Wise.
"Enthusiasm is caught not taught."

Encouragement

Here are today's Words to the Wise.
"Lift people up!"

Reality

Here are today's Words to the Wise.
"If the shoe fits. . ."

Peace on Earth

Here are today's Words to the Wise.
"Peace begins with us."

Time

Here are today's Words to the Wise.
"Work while you wait."

Goals

Here are today's Words to the Wise.
"Aim High."

Intellect

Here are today's Words to the Wise.
"Keep your mind busy."

Quality

Here are today's Words to the Wise.
"Vow to make a difference in your life."

Grateful

Here are today's Words to the Wise.
"Remember to say thank you."

New Life

Here are today's Words to the Wise.
"Every end is a beginning."

Judging

Here are today's Words to the Wise.
"A pearl is often found in an ugly shell."

Integrity

Here are today's Words to the Wise.
"Your character is your destiny."

Real Freedom

Here are today's Words to the Wise. "Education can help to set you free."

Reliable

Here are today's Words to the Wise.
"Keep your word."

Expression

Here are today's Words to the Wise.
"Singing is good for the soul."

Giving Thanks

Here are today's Words to the Wise.
"Develop a thankful heart."

Life Lessons

Here are today's Words to the Wise.
"Experience is a hard teacher."

Time Management

Here are today's Words to the Wise.
"Work while you wait."

Welcoming

Here are today's Words to the Wise.
"Eat lunch with the new kids."

Circulation

Here are today's Words to the Wise.
"Receive by giving."

Faith

Here are today's Words to the Wise.
"It pays to believe in miracles."

Joy

Here are today's Words to the Wise.
"Laugh Out Loud!"

Courage

Here are today's Words to the Wise.
"If you don't ask, you don't get."

Encouragement

Here are today's Words to the Wise.
"Life is not necessarily fair,
but it's still good."

Fired up!

Here are today's Words to the Wise.
"Stay ready so you don't have to get ready."
—Thanks to BJ Waymer!

Meditation

Here are today's Words to the Wise.
"Set aside quiet time each day."

Healing

Here are today's Words to the Wise.
"Allow peace to come through."

Inspire

Here are today's Words to the Wise.
"Read for inspiration."

Uplifting

Here are today's Words to the Wise.
"Good words cost nothing. Share them."

Optimism

Here are today's Words to the Wise.
"The future is now."

Ability

Here are today's Words to the Wise.
"Know your Limitations."

Inspiration

Here are today's Words to the Wise.
"Your dreams are
more valuable than money."

Empathy

Here are today's Words to the Wise.
"Take the time to listen...with your heart."

Affirm

Here are today's Words to the Wise.
"Be willing to be your authentic self."

Integrity

Here are today's Words to the Wise.
"Pay what you owe."

Honor

Here are today's Words to the Wise.
"Appreciate one another."

Quality

Here are today's Words to the Wise.
"Double-check your work."

Re-Start

Here are today's Words to the Wise.
"Re-invent yourself."

Value

Here are today's Words to the Wise.
"Yesterday will never come again,
but we have today."

Grace

Here are today's Words to the Wise.
"Give thanks for your food."

Power

Here are today's Words to the Wise.
"In Unity there is strength."

Love

Here are today's Words to the Wise.
"Dare yourself to love more."

Education

Here are today's Words to the Wise.
"Education is the great equalizer."

Expectations

Here are today's Words to the Wise.
"Promise little and do much."

Heart

Here are today's Words to the Wise.
"Forgiving someone is a sign of strength."

Joy

Here are today's Words to the Wise.
"There's always room for happiness."

Hope

Here are today's Words to the Wise.
"You Can."

Prosperity

Here are today's Words to the Wise.
"Great people do great things;
know that you're great."

Wisdom

Here are today's Words to the Wise.
"Listen and Learn."

Joy

Here are today's Words to the Wise.
"Busy People have more fun."

Inspiration

Here are today's Words to the Wise
"To hope is to live."

Wisdom

Here are today's Words to the Wise.
"If it isn't broken, improve it."

Change

Here are today's Words to the Wise.
"Progress begins with a dream."

Rise Above

Here are today's Words to the Wise.
"Soar with the Eagles!!"

High Road

Here are today's Words to the Wise.
"Rise above the little things."

Caring

Here are today's Words to the Wise.
"You gain when you give of yourself."

Self-Aware

Here are today's Words to the Wise.
"Be who you are."

Joy

Here are today's Words to the Wise.
"Make it a point to laugh more."

Compassion

Here are today's Words to the Wise.
"Have a tender heart."

Power

Here are today's Words to the Wise.
"I have the capacity to succeed!"

In Present Moment

Here are today's Words to the Wise.
"It's okay just to be."

Begin Again

Here are today's Words to the Wise.
"Every day is a clean slate."

Relationships

Here are today's Words to the Wise.
"You can't buy friendship."

Real Love

Here are today's Words to the Wise
"Love has a life of its own."

Vision

Here are today's Words to the Wise.
"Dream Big Dreams."

Wealth

Here are today's Words to the Wise.
"A wealthy person is one
who enjoys each day."

Who's Listening?

Here are today's Words to the Wise.
"Little children have big ears."

What Mom Says!

Here are today's Words to the Wise.
"Mind Your Business."

Soaring

Here are today's Words to the Wise.
"Allow your dreams to live."

Tact

Here are today's Words to the Wise.
"Not everything should be said."

Integrity

Here are today's Words to the Wise.
"Your character is your destiny."

Real Power

Here are today's Words to the Wise.
"Love has the power to change things."

Alignment

Here are today's Words to the Wise.
"Put your house in order."

Compassion

Here are today's Words to the Wise.
"Have a tender heart."

Obtainable Goal

Here are today's Words to the Wise.
"Strive for Excellence."

Financial Health

Here are today's Words to the Wise.
"Save Money!"

Mental Agility

Here are today's Words to the Wise.
"Use your mind as a tool."

Real

Here are today's Words to the Wise.
"True beauty doesn't need to be dressed up."

Individuality

Here are today's Words to the Wise.
"Every person is unique."

Reflections

Here are today's Words to the Wise.
"Listen to your feelings."

Partnership

Here are today's Words to the Wise.
"Don't be afraid to ask for help."

Caring

Here are today's Words to the Wise.
"Make forgiveness a practice."

Calm

Here are today's Words to the Wise.
"Patience achieves more than Force."

Centering

Here are today's Words to the Wise.
"Life is a balancing act."

Start

Here are today's Words to the Wise.
"Begin where you are."

Balance

Here are today's Words to the Wise.
"Live within your income."

Life

Here are today's Words to the Wise.
"Life is meant for living."

Appreciation

Here are today's Words to the Wise.
"Enjoy the journey as much as the stay."

Heart

Here are today's Words to the Wise.
"Dare yourself to love more."

Honesty

Here are today's Words to the Wise.
"When in doubt tell the truth."

Life

Here are today's Words to the Wise.
"The meaning of life is to find meaning."

Integrity

Here are today's Words to the Wise.
"Honesty rules the day!"

Freedom

Here are today's Words to the Wise.
"Real freedom isn't easily attained."

Real Happiness

Here are today's Words to the Wise.
"Happiness is more than riches."

Alert

Here are today's Words to the Wise.
"Look for opportunities."

Power

Here are today's Words to the Wise.
"In unity there is strength."

Strength

Here are today's Words to the Wise.
"Love is the heart's power."

Humor

Here are today's Words to the Wise.
"Well-placed humor can add
spice to your life."

No Boundaries

Here are today's Words to the Wise.
"Go Beyond Your Limitations."

Selflessness

Here are today's Words to the Wise.
"Dare to open your heart."

Dreams

Here are today's Words to the Wise.
"Do what you love."

Unpredictability

Here are today's Words to the Wise.
"It's always something."

Real Freedom

Here are today's Words to the Wise.
"Education sets you free."

Observe

Here are today's Words to the Wise.
"Watch, listen, understand."

Life

Here are today's Words to the Wise.
"History teaches by example."

Love

Here are today's Words to the Wise.
"Love knows no boundaries."

Certainty

Here are today's Words to the Wise.
"Nothing endures like change."

Vision

Here are today's Words to the Wise.
"A person with vision sees the invisible."

Love Secret

Here are today's Words to the Wise.
"If you want to be loved, then love."

Brain Power

Here are today's Words to the Wise.
"Genius is thinking in an unusual way."

Think

Here are today's Words to the Wise.
"Be led by reason."

Vision

Here are today's Words to the Wise.
"See more than what your eyes show you."

Real Joy

Here are today's Words to the Wise.
"Find joy in the simple things."

Effectiveness

Here are today's Words to the Wise.
"Your very best is good enough."

Speech

Here are today's Words to the Wise.
"Speak words that are true,
kind and constructive."

Character

Here are today's Words to the Wise.
"Be tough-minded but tender-hearted."

Listen

Here are today's Words to the Wise.
"Be willing to hear the other side."

Greatness

Here are today's Words to the Wise.
"Expect unprecedented favor in your life."

Wealth

Here are today's Words to the Wise.
"Good health is true wealth."

Inner-Joy

Here are today's Words to the Wise.
"Enthusiasm is as contagious
as the common cold."

Forgive

Here are today's Words to the Wise.
"Forgive Yourself."

Instinct

Here are today's Words to the Wise.
"Trust your judgement."

Unlimited

Here are today's Words to the Wise.
"Our capacities are greater than we imagine."

Education

Here are today's Words to the Wise.
"Life is about Learning."

Love

Here are today's Words to the Wise.
"Love who you are."

Benevolence

Here are today's Words to the Wise.
"A generous act is its own reward."

Ego Check

Here are today's words to the Wise.
"Don't dismiss a good idea just because
you don't like where it came from."

Attitude

Here are today's Words to the Wise.
"Coolness comes naturally to cool people."

High Road

Here are today's Words to the Wise.
"Take a wider view."

Positive

Here are today's Words to the Wise.
"Look for opportunities to
praise and appreciate."

Knowing

Here are today's Words to the Wise.
"Trust your instincts."

Value

Here are today's Words to the Wise.
"What is useful will last; what is
hurtful will sink."

Persevere

Here are today's Words to the Wise.
"No one ever said it would be easy."

Life Lessons

Here are today's Words to the Wise.
"Adversity can be a great teacher."

Time

Here are today's Words to the Wise.
"Time is a state of mind."

Security

Here are today's Words to the Wise.
"Get it in writing."

Truth

Here are today's Words to the Wise.
"Nothing is lost when you seek the truth."

Laughter

Here are today's Words to The Wise.
"Humor is the spice of life."

Planning

Here are today's Words to the Wise.
"Timing is Everything."

Life

Here are today's Words to the Wise.
"You become what's in your heart."

Emotions

Here are today's Words to the Wise.
"The thinnest line is between love and hate."

Imagination

Here are today's Words to the Wise.
"Go confidently in
the direction of your dreams."

Confidence

Here are today's Words to the Wise.
"Truly believing in yourself is a skill."

Secret

Here are today's Words to the Wise.
"The key to freedom is in our minds."

Wise

Here are today's Words to the Wise.
"There's no such thing as
too much common sense."

Treasures

Here are today's Words to the Wise.
"Wealth is a state of mind."

Power

Here are today's Words to the Wise.
"Strength comes from commitment."

Impact

Here are today's Words to the Wise.
"Your ability to change, changes the world."

Quality

Here are today's Words to the Wise.
"Do little things well."

Real Love

Here are today's Words to the Wise.
"Love begins from within."

Arbiter

Here are today's Words to the Wise.
"The best judge of an argument is time."

Highest Good

Here are today's Words to the Wise.
"God is in the Details."

Maximize

Here are today's Words to the Wise.
"Believe in unlimited potential."

Now

Here are today's Words to the Wise.
"There is no future like the present."

Details

Here are today's Words to the Wise.
"Read the fine print!"

Peace

Here are today's Words to the Wise.
"Don't carry grudges."

Wisdom

Here are today's Words to the Wise.
"There are many branches
to the Tree of Knowledge."

Setbacks

Here are today's Words to the Wise.
"Mistakes are opportunities to learn."

Accolades

Here are today's Words to the Wise.
"Excellence is its own reward."

Respect

Here are today's Words to the Wise.
"Acknowledge a gift, no matter how small."

Standards

Here are today's Words to the Wise.
"Don't compromise your integrity."

Life Lesson

Here are today's Words to the Wise.
"Forgiveness is the ultimate lesson."

Sharing

Here are today's Words to the Wise.
"List three things you're thankful for
and share your list with family or friends."

Thankful

Here are today's Words to the Wise.
"A thankful heart is a great virtue."

Heart

Here are today's Words to the Wise.
"Be kind to the unkind."

True Gift

Here are today's Words to the Wise.
"Optimism is a gift."

Happy

Here are today's Words to the Wise.
"The time to be happy is now."

Guidance

Here are today's Words to the Wise.
"Be your child's best teacher and coach."

Success

Here are today's Words to the Wise.
"Successful people are made not born."

Love

Here are today's Words to the Wise.
"Love conquers hate."

Wisdom

Here are today's Words to the Wise.
"Keep your own counsel."

Faith

Here are today's Words to the Wise.
"Life is all about dealing with the unknowns."

Right Action

Here are today's Words to the Wise.
"Peace is goodwill in action."

Restraint

Here are today's Words to the Wise.
"Know when to stop."

Manners

Here are today's Words to the Wise.
"Good guests know when to leave."

Listen

Here are today's Words to the Wise.
"You can win more friends with
your ears than with your mouth."

Fresh Start

Here are today's Words to the Wise.
"Tomorrow is a new day!"

Value

Here are today's Words to the Wise.
"Don't sell yourself short."

Well-Being

Here are today's Words to the Wise.
"Be a friend to yourself first."

Empathy

Here are today's Words to the Wise.
"Care enough to listen."

Honor

Here are today's Words to the Wise.
"Never forget an act of kindness."

Goals

Here are today's Words to the Wise.
"Aim for success, not perfection."

Righteousness

Here are today's Words to the Wise.
"You can't fake integrity."

Wisdom

Here are today's Words to the Wise.
"There's no such thing as
too much common sense."

Freedom

Here are today's Words to the Wise.
"Freedom has responsibility."

Joy

Here are today's Words to the Wise.
"Remember to laugh and smile."

True Wealth

Here are today's Words to the Wise.
"To know when you have
enough is to be rich."

Education

Here are today's Words to the Wise.
"A good education requires more
than just going to school."

Empathy

Here are today's Words to the Wise.
"Care enough to listen."

Decisions

Here are today's Words to the Wise.
"Making the right choices takes a
great deal of courage."

Receptive

Here are today's Words to the Wise.
"If opportunity knocks, let her in."

Now Moment

Here are today's Words to the Wise.
"Nothing is worth more than this day."

Friendship

Here are today's Words to the Wise.
"A true friend never gets in
your way unless you're going down."

Wisdom

Here are today's Words to the Wise.
"Stop trying to control the uncontrollable."

Support

Here are today's Words to the Wise.
"Encourage anyone trying to improve."

Connect

Here are today's Words to the Wise.
"Keep the communication lines open."

Strength

Here are today's Words to the Wise.
"I stand strong with a mighty faith."

Rigor

Here are today's Words to the Wise.
"Strive for Excellence."

Action

Here are today's Words to the Wise.
"I know that the future is now."

Giving

Here are today's Words to the Wise.
"Give with joy and joy is your reward."

Trust

Here are today's Words to the Wise.
"Seemingly tough situations
have a way of working out."

Opportunity

Here are today's Words to the Wise.
"Luck, if you believe in it, favors
those who are prepared."

Discernment

Here are today's Words to the Wise.
"There is a difference
between news and gossip. "

Peace

Here are today's Words to the Wise.
"Search for the secret of tranquility."

Press On

Here are today's Words to the Wise.
"Don't let fear hold you back."

Power

Here are today's Words to the Wise.
"Hope gives a person strength."

Seeing

Here are today's Words to the Wise.
"Open your eyes to the miracles
that happen everyday."

Family

Here are today's Words to the Wise.
"Share the remote control."

Shallow

Here are today's Words to the Wise.
"There's a big difference
between words and actions."

Courage

Here are today's Words to the Wise.
"Worry doesn't solve a damn thing.
Hard work and dogged determination do."

Internal

Here are today's Words to the Wise.
"Success has a lot to do with attitude."

You're Human

Here are today's Words to the Wise.
"Don't be discouraged by your mistakes."

Heart

Here are today's Words to the Wise.
"Life is a song to sing. I vow to
sing a beautiful melody."

Beauty

Here are today's Words to the Wise.
"Everyone is beautiful when they smile."

Choices

Here are today's Words to the Wise.
"Life is what you make it; choose wisely."

Productivity

Here are today's Words to the Wise.
"Ideas never work unless you do."

Success

Here are today's Words to the Wise.
"Act like the person you want to be."

Worry

Here are today's Words to the Wise.
"Most of the things we worry
about never happen."

Courage

Here are today's Words to the Wise.
"We usually know the right thing to do;
the hardest part is doing it."

Civility

Here are today's Words to the Wise.
"Respond to rudeness with kindness."

Productivity

Here are today's Words to the Wise.
"Know the difference between
being at work and working."

Clarity

Here are today's Words to the Wise.
"People often condemn that which
they don't understand."

Success

Here are today's Words to the Wise.
"The key to failure is trying
to please everyone."

Secrets

Here are today's Words to the Wise.
"If only one knows it, it is a secret;
if two know it, it is public."

Honesty

Here are today's Words to the Wise.
"A lie can never fix the truth."

Moving Forward

Here are today's Words to the Wise.
"While you can't change the past,
you can influence the future."

Efficiency

Here are today's Words to the Wise.
"If you want something done,
ask a busy person." —Ben Franklin

Blessings

Here are today's Words to the Wise.
"Good health and good sense
are two of life's greatest blessings."

Balance

Here are today's Words to the Wise.
"Give a little, take a little."

Life

Here are today's Words to the Wise.
"Life is 10 percent what happens to you
and 90 percent how you react to it."

Value

Here are today's Words to the Wise.
"Life is a coin you can only spend once."

Our Words

Here are today's Words to the Wise.
"Praise twice as much as you criticize."

Limits

Here are today's Words to the Wise.
"Know when enough is enough."

Adversity

Here are today's Words to the Wise.
"Adversity is a great teacher."

Rewards

Here are today's Words to the Wise.
"Doing something right is reward enough."

Dream Big

Here are today's Words to the Wise.
"What you do is limited only
by what you can dream."

The Gift

Here are today's Words to the Wise.
"Find the extraordinary in the ordinary."

Open Mind

Here are today's Words to the Wise.
"An open mind supports an open heart."

Strength

Here are today's Words to the Wise. "Nothing is so strong as gentleness; nothing is so gentle as real strength."

Optimism

Here are today's Words to the Wise.
"The optimist sees opportunity
in every difficulty."

Passion

Here are today's Words to the Wise.
"Passion is an important key to success."

Freedom

Here are today's Words to the Wise.
"Intelligence brings Freedom."

You're Great

Here are today's Words to the Wise.
"Don't sell yourself short!"

Now

Here are today's Words to the Wise.
"There is no future like the present."

New

Here are today's Words to the Wise.
"I open myself to new experiences
that may enrich my life."

Good Friday

Here are today's Words to the Wise.
"Count your blessings."

Ease

Here are today's Words to the Wise.
"Simplify."

Encouragement

Here are today's Words to the Wise.
"You were born to succeed!"

Optimistic

Here are today's Words to the Wise.
"Life is an uncertain voyage."

Caution

Here are today's Words to the Wise.
"Take one step at a time."

Grateful

Here are today's Words to the Wise.
"Pleasure is gained by giving"

Self-Care

Here are today's Words to the Wise.
"Recharge if you need to."

Moderation

Here are today's Words to the Wise.
"Less is more."

Moderation

Here are today's Words to the Wise.
"Nothing in excess!"

Encouragement

Here are today's Words to the Wise.
"You can, we can."

Today

Here are today's Words to the Wise.
"Today is the day!!"

Ease

Here are today's Words to the Wise.
"Simplify."

Encouragement

Here are today's Words to the Wise.
"You were born to succeed!"

Optimistic

Here are today's Words to the Wise.
"Life is an uncertain voyage."

Caution

Here are today's Words to the Wise.
"Take one step at a time."

Grateful

Here are today's Words to the Wise.
"Pleasure is gained by giving."

Self-Care

Here are today's Words to the Wise.
"Recharge if you need to."

Moderation

Here are today's Words to the Wise.
"Less is more."

Moderation

Here are today's Words to the Wise.
"Nothing in excess!"

Encouragement

Here are today's Words to the Wise.
"You can, we can."

Empathy

Here are today's Words to the Wise.
"Listen with your eyes."

Envy

Here are today's Words to the Wise.
"Forget about the Joneses."

Calm

Here are today's Words to the Wise.
"Practice patience."

Life

Here are today's Words to the Wise.
"Every day is a lifetime."

Share

Here are today's Words to the Wise.
"Beware, kindness is contagious."

Love

Here are today's Words to the Wise.
"Love is a gift."

Respect

Here are today's Words to the Wise.
"Courtesy never goes out of style."

Abundance

Here are today's Words to the Wise.
"Less is More!"

Action

Here are today's Words to the Wise.
"Doing can be better than saying."

Presence

Here are today's Words to the Wise.
"Live in the Now Moment."

Well-Being

Here are today's Words to the Wise.
"Good health...priceless!"

Giving

Here are today's Words to the Wise.
"Forgive and forget."

Honor

Here are today's Words to the Wise.
"A kind word goes a long way."

Clear Vision

Here are today's Words to the Wise.
"Reality isn't an illusion."

Expand

Here are today's Words to the Wise.
"Allow joy in your life!"

Efficiency

Here are today's Words to the Wise.
"Work smart!"

Self-Value

Here are today's Words to the Wise.
"Invest in Yourself."

Joy

Here are today's Words to the Wise.
"Live out Loud!"

Empathy

Here are today's Words to the Wise.
"Seek to Understand."

Self-Confidence

Here are today's Words to the Wise.
"Think for yourself."

Perseverance

Here are today's Words to the Wise.
"Rise Up!"